Ray's Radishes

written & illustrated by
Tatyana Eckstrand

Furry Purry Press
Waldoboro, ME

Furry Purry Press

Ray's Radishes / written & illustrated by Tatyana Eckstrand

Copyright ©2016 by Tatyana Eckstrand

Published by:
Furry Purry Press
514 Duck Puddle Rd.
Waldoboro, ME 04572

Publisher's Cataloging-In-Publication Data
(Prepared by The Donohue Group, Inc.)

Names: Eckstrand, Tatyana, author, illustrator.
Title: Ray's radishes / written & illustrated by Tatyana Eckstrand.
Description: Waldoboro, ME : Furry Purry Press, [2016] | Interest age level: 003-010. | Summary: Take a tour through the vegetable garden with Farmer Ray. He'll show you lots of different vegetables and even tell you which one is his favorite! Follow along with the fun limerick rhyme."--Provided by publisher.
Identifiers: ISBN 978-0-692-64005-0
Subjects: LCSH: Vegetables--Juvenile fiction. | Vegetable gardening--Juvenile fiction. | Farmers--Juvenile fiction. | Stories in rhyme. CYAC: Vegetables--Fiction. | Vegetable gardening--Fiction. | Farmers--Fiction.
Classification: LCC PZ7.1.E35 Ra 2016 | DDC [E]--dc23

Printed in the United States of America

*In memory of Papa
and his wonderful garden.*

There lives a farmer named Ray
Who plants a big garden each May.
He waters the seeds
And pulls all the weeds
And his veggies grow bigger each day.

He shows friends how his plants grew.
He shows them to visitors, too.
Ray takes them through rows,
Even shows them the hose.
Now he'll show his garden to you!

"Do you know what these are? Can you tell?
These are onions; they taste really swell.
They're white and they're round
And they grow in the ground.
Eat them raw and your breath will smell!"

"This orange one, this is a carrot.
You silly head, no, you don't wear it!
It's long and it's sweet
And it's fun to eat
Especially when you share it!"

"Have you ever heard of bok choy?
I loved it when I was a boy!
It has stalks that are white
And green leaves; take a bite!
Oh, seeing it grow is a joy!"

"Potatoes I mash, fry, or bake.
But how many of these can I take?
They're brown with some spots,
And each plant grows lots.
Oh, I've picked them 'til my back does ache!"

"This cabbage," Ray said, "is great raw!
Chew it lots; it's good for your jaw.
It looks round as a ball
And, no, that's not all--
If you grate it, you've made cole slaw!"

"Now squash grows on long curly vines.
They love it lots when the sun shines!
Squash makes me feel good.
I'd eat more if I could."
(Ray <u>often</u> has squash when he dines.)

"This vegetable is named broccoli.
When it's cut, it looks like a tree.
If you use it in soup,
It tastes better than goop.
And it looks better, too ... Hee! Hee!"

"I admit that this celery looks weird.
The first time it sprouted I cheered!
See the green stalks grow tall.
But the leaves are so small."
Ray said as he scratched at his beard.

"This daikon is something real new.
I have grown it a year or two.
They're like carrots but white,
And bigger. What a sight!
And they taste like radishes do!"

"I've been husking this since I was born,
And so now my poor gloves are worn.
Look at that, fine fellow,
The kernels are yellow,
And the ears are green-- yes, it's corn!"

"My wife planted lettuce, I'm guessing.
She loves it in salad with dressing.
With green leaves that are thin,
They make sandwiches grin.
Oh, each bit of food is a blessing!"

"You can see I grow all kinds of beans:
Such as long, short, and fat-in-betweens.
They're eaten by bums,
By anyone who hums,
And they're eaten by kings and queens!"

Now Ray's favorite are small and red.
"These are radishes!" Farmer Ray said.
"When there's no one around,
I gobble them down,
And think, 'I don't need lunch; I've been fed!'"

"Cauliflower is a hard white puff
And picking it's really quite tough.
It's surrounded by leaves,"
Then Ray pulled up his sleeves
And said, "Whew! I've shown you enough!"

A farmer's work never is done,
But Ray loves being out in the sun.
He'll sing and he'll sow,
And he'll dance with his hoe,
And he'll laugh and shout, "Wow, this is fun!"

Ray knows that his garden is blessed.
It thrives when it's put to the test.
All the squash is so sweet,
And carrots are a treat,
But his radishes-- Ray likes the BEST!

Made in the USA
Monee, IL
07 July 2026